Terms and Conditions

LEGAL NOTICE

The Publisher has strived to be as accurate and complete as possible in the creation of this report, notwithstanding the fact that he does not warrant or represent at any time that the contents within are accurate due to the rapidly changing nature of the Internet.

While all attempts have been made to verify information provided in this publication, the Publisher assumes no responsibility for errors, omissions, or contrary interpretation of the subject matter herein. Any perceived slights of specific persons, peoples, or organizations are unintentional.

In practical advice books, like anything else in life, there are no guarantees of income made. Readers are cautioned to reply on their own judgment about their individual circumstances to act accordingly.

This book is not intended for use as a source of legal, business, accounting or financial advice. All readers are advised to seek services of competent professionals in legal, business, accounting and finance fields.

You are encouraged to print this book for easy reading.

Table Of Contents

Foreword

Chapter 1:
Introduction

Chapter 2:
What is Traffic Generation?

Chapter 3:
Traffic Generation and Personality Type

Chapter 4:
Winning Strategies for a Traffic Generation

Chapter 5:
The Characteristics of Good and Stable Traffic

Chapter 6:
Factors to Consider in Choosing a TrafficGeneration for You

Chapter 7:
Assessment Parameters for a WorkingGenerator

Chapter 8:
Value Based Returns from Traffic

Chapter 9:
The Value of Traffic

Wrapping Up
The Value of Traffic

Foreword

This "course" was put together to help you get maximum benefits from your online marketing activities is composed of ten chapters. After you have gone over it or have undergone it, it is expected that you have acquired adequate knowledge on what traffic is, how it is generated, the various traffic generating strategies available these days and which of them suit you best.

Chapter 1 WHIch is the introductory part, answers the questions: what is traffic and types of traffic. Afterwards, you will be given a preview of the contents of the succeeding chapters.
Get all the info you need here.

The Traffic Generation Personality Type

Discover What Traffic Generation Strategies Are Suitable for You

Chapter 1:
Introduction

Synopsis

Traffic is the number of number of people who visit your online sites. If you website is for business, you hope to convert the traffic into sales. This means that driving traffic to your sites is one of the crucial activities you have to do in order to achieve internet market success.

The Basics

Basically, there are three types of online traffic: paid traffic, free traffic and earned traffic.

Paid Online Traffic – Online marketers want their marketing activities to be targeted so they pay for the services of networks and agencies that will help them find best and most effective online advertizing strategies. One of the most important ad strategies is the pay per click or PPC advertizing.

(1) PPC - This method allows you to place ads in the search results generated by search engines that used the targeted keywords you specified in your campaign. You pay a certain amount every time a searcher clicks on your ads and visits your website.

(2) CPM – In this method, it is presumed that a searcher has seen your ad in the website where ad happens to in. When a thousand visitors have "seen" you are billed a certain amount. The amount depends on the bid you have placed with the network.

(3) CPV – Cost per View is another paid online advertizing method becoming increasingly popular. What you do is submit to the network of choice your capture page or website, supply your target market and keywords, and for a

fee, the network will direct traffic generated by the keywords to either to your website or capture page.

There are other forms of advertizing, but these three are the most important these days.

Free Online Traffic simply means you do not have to pay money upfront for advertizing. You can use the free online advertizing sites like Backpage and Craiglist. You can also use the social media networks like YouTube, Facebook, and twitter. There is Ad Swap which is basically forging partnerships with other websites. You advertize your partner's products in your website and he does the same for your products in his own site.

Earned Traffic is the traffic you get after hours, days and even months of writing and posting innumerable SEO loaded blogs to your website and website directories. It can also be the result of word of mouth where staff and satisfied customers spread the word that your products or services are good.

After having reviewed what traffic is all about and the various ways of generating it, let's go through the rest of the material.

Chapter 2 answers the question: What is traffic generation? Which will be most helpful when you are deciding the kind of traffic you will want to have.

Chapter 3 discusses what kind of traffic generation will be suitable for you based on your inclinations, situation and needs.

Chapter 4 discusses strategies whether you are going for free or paid traffic.

Chapter 5 discusses the characteristics of good and stable traffic. Obviously, some traffic is useless or can dry up.

Chapter 6 discusses the factors that you should consider when choosing the type and strategy for campaigns.

Chapter 7 discusses the criteria for assessing the effectiveness of your strategy.

Chapter 8 discusses the returns on investment of such campaigns as PPCs.

Chapter 9 stresses the importance of traffic for generating sales and provides some valuable tips on traffic generation.

Chapter 10 is a simple case study that tells about a website owner's experiences about traffic generation. You will learn a lot of lessons from it.

Chapter 2:

What is Traffic Generation?

Synopsis

So you've managed to put together a beautiful and compelling landing page or website now what? Where are you going to get the visitors from?

As website owners we of course need quality prospects which mean the visitor is perfectly matched with the product or service being offered at the website. The objective of traffic generation is to get as many targeted visitors to your website preferably through free traffic sources, however if you can afford it, you can go get paid traffic such as Adwords and similar services, Banners, CPA, Joint venture campaigns etc.

Free traffic is better economically although it is not really free unless you do the SEO yourself, or past efforts are now paying off, your website naturally is getting traffic from every source, without lifting a finger.

Where to Get Traffic Online

Practically anywhere on the Internet can be used as a traffic generator. You can get traffic by posting pictures to websites like Pinterest, Flickr, deviant art, Instagram even pictures uploaded to Google images with your watermark showing your website.

Through Search engine optimization or by getting your websites to rank for keywords (that in your estimate will target the most ideal prospects) has become harder recently because of Google's obsession to quality of visitor experience. Unless you have been in the Internet marketing game or SEO for a very long time this might prove difficult especially to novices.

Other Sources of Online Traffic

Video traffic also nowadays is becoming increasing harder to do. Bulk video uploads of low-quality get removed fairly easily in YouTube and similar sites. If you have excellent videos that actually give value to the viewers, and has the potential to be viral, this can prove to be a good free traffic source for a long time.

Commenting On Blogs and Forums

Not only does this improve your sites SEO or search engine optimization, it allows you to capture much targeted prospects and as

an added benefit you can get the pulse and feedback of the things going on in your industry.

Article Marketing

Though considered an old-school method to get free traffic, it's still effective and pulls visitors. The same principle applies by writing good quality it has the potential to be viral and will generate click through to your website.

Social Media Marketing

Social sites such as Facebook, Twitter, bookmarking sites and other online hangouts can produce direct traffic to your website posting your links in these sites.

In terms of SEO Google's giving a lot of importance to what is called social signals which in the updated Google algorithm, a sign of a good website (worthy of high rankings) is that a lot of people are talking about it and posting its links everywhere. The objective is not only to get your sites scattered all over the Internet, but for it to have a life of its own by becoming viral.

Vitality is the name of the game and you can only achieve it if the content is valuable enough that people on their own want to share it with their friends.

Email Marketing

Visitors you can get when your sites are recommended by marketers with their own email lists. You can either promote your websites on your own this that you have developed or bought over the years, or you can find a joint venture partner in possession of a big list to promote your websites, usually in exchange for a cut of the profits.

Chapter 3:
Traffic Generation and Personality Type

Synopsis

There are an infinite number of ways to generate traffic-quality or just general traffic (Perhaps because you need to have a high Alexa ratings and any traffic whether it converts or not is beneficial).

As an Internet marketer you may prefer to be involved with certain activities online over others. Some like to hang out at YouTube and other video sites, while others just enjoy writing a bunch of content either for their blogs, or for public dissemination in article sites, Web 2.0's, Wiki etc.

How Personal Preference Affects Traffic Generation Efforts

In general it is advisable to be tapped into many traffic sources as possible, and for those sections on the Internet that you do not enjoy doing personally, you may task it to a partner or a virtual assistant.

A lot of online marketers actually employed more of black hat marketing before, which used to mean rubbish, low quality in vast quantities made and disseminated using automation tools.

Because of the Google crackdown on sites using automation and automatic posting of texts, black hat now means automation but the quality has now drastically improved. There are of course other black hat methods still available and work to a limited extent.

The Person Who Enjoys Making Online Connections and Relationships

For those who enjoy making relationships, they tap into email marketing more than others. It is indeed one of the better traffic sources as the traffic is highly targeted and relationship building is factored in, as well as longer term value building of the products.

Though for some reason people who enjoy the anonymity on the Internet avoid making personal connections online whenever they can. A lot of Internet marketers do not do email campaigns though it

has been proven to be effective in generating sales and long-term customer relationships and they know it!

People buy because of the relationship at times over the intrinsic merits of the product itself, so you may want to get into this even if it seems intimidating at first.

Another variation of personal relationship contact online which surprisingly is comfortable for many is Facebook, Twitter and others.

Facebook has become a regularly part of many people's lives that it can now be utilized to directly communicate with the customers and prospects that may not always check or are receptive to the communications coursed through emails.

It boils down to personal preference; email marketing does tend to be more impersonal than Facebook for some. However other complicated metrics, and the very nature of the marketing message are not possible in Facebook, which are only possible through other means like email- making it irreplaceable.

Pictures, Sounds and Videos in Online Traffic Generation

A new trend that has started popping up this recent years are picture sharing sites like deviant art, Pinterest, Flickr, Instagram etc. These sites allow people to share and comment on their own and other people's pictures. This attracts the graphic artists, photographers the most, or anyone who just loves viewing, manipulating and taking pictures.

For the audiophiles, there are sites like Sound casts and podcasts sites that allow people to listen and broadcast their messages in audio form.

If audio and static pictures or writings are still not enough and does not appeal to the online marketer's personality, they may perhaps prefer to speak directly to the individual by creating videos and because everyone has high-speed broadband internet nowadays, arguably this mode of communication is the most convenient and preferred by majority of the Netizens.

If however the presentations are too long, many will still prefer written texts i.e. blog posts, articles, e-books, as they can save a lot of time soaking in the message without having to read through everything (speed reading).

In conclusion, if you intend to do the traffic generation efforts yourself, find what you love, do as much of it as you can, without neglecting the other sources of traffic by outsourcing those tasks to others.

Chapter 4:

Winning Strategies for Traffic Generation

Synopsis

As discussed in the previous chapter, due to the multitude of available traffic sources online, people tend to stick to just a few traffic generation methods while neglecting others that do not interest them or prove too cumbersome.

A winning strategy for traffic generation is to leave no stone unturned! Any and all sources of traffic must be tapped and utilized to arrive with as much quality and quantity traffic to your website. Getting good conversions depends on quality or laser-targeted visitors who want to buy or use the product/services being offered on your website.

Quantity or sources of traffic that are not as good, are usually funneled through a different sales process (assuming you are selling a product or service) such as when you want to send them freebies, getting them to be on your email list to start the relationship building or the sales process-by getting a small compliance to get them invested, better informed and interested for future sales.

Short Term Traffic Strategies

You can generate quick bursts of traffic by conducting special promotions, when any of your videos/content suddenly becomes viral etc. The nature of it being short term, the next day traffic may just dry up.

There are many tactics and strategies to generate short-term traffic like this. Examples are black hat tactics usually only to get quick surge of visitors, that do not generally last. The blogs, video sites and other public sites may take down your posts upon discovery due to its poor quality.

Long Term Traffic Strategies

Long-term traffic tactics is about producing good, quality, bulletproof content that Google and other public web properties do not get rid of.

Long-term traffic takes into account good risk management, diversification of your website properties, factoring in that some websites will simply not make it and are designed to support the primary website to rank higher in the long run-to slowly and carefully climb up in the rankings as a stable source of traffic.

Because search engine optimization factors in the organic or natural looking patterns of link building from these supporting websites, they cannot be blasted all at once, as it will trigger a red flag on the search engines.

The web properties promoting the main website must also have support websites promoting the traffic feeders surrounding it.

In essence, it's about building a network of websites supporting other members of the network encompassing all of the possible web properties, whether it be a bookmark, an article site, a wiki, blogs, or video sites. It can also come in the form of podcasts, RSS, e-book sites, forums, social media, image sharing sites, file sharing sites, and every imaginable place you can drop links, or get direct traffic either to the main website, or to a satellite site in support of the main website.

Chapter 5:
The Characteristics of Good and Stable Traffic

Synopsis

Producing website traffic is one part of the business success. If there is no continuous flow of visitors, you may not be able to sell successfully. Traffic is another component to consider so you can offer your services or sell your products. It can help your business gain more popularity and visibility.

Having a beautifully designed website is not good enough when there is no amount of traffic coming in. To ensure your visitors are attracted always give something of value. The next step to take seriously after making a website is generating your traffic

How to Get More Traffic

Here are some characteristics of traffic that are consistent and visible online.

1. *Have something valuable to offer.*

There's no better way to keep visitors from coming back than having something beneficial for them. Therefore, each post must be of great value to teach people something new. Do not attempt to write an article post filled with a bunch of fillers to increase the number of words. If your content is fresh, informative and vibrant, your visitors will go back to your site for more, and they will like it, share it, link it, email it, tweet about it, and more. It means more traffic can be generated.

2. *Join with other related blogs.*

Search for the top 10 or top 5 blogs with the same niche of your website then be one of the active commenter's. Read two or three posts every week and share your thoughts about it. When leaving comments, you can start leaving a link to your website. If your comments are good and interesting, many other visitors will go to your website.

3. *Be genuinely aggressive.*

If you want to have a growing traffic, you need to be aggressive with your attempt to generate some methods to improve your traffic. You can't just post several articles or submit some videos and wait for overflowing traffic. It doesn't easily work fast that way. First is to be filled with passion while working hard on your traffic. Submit as

much informative and valuable articles as possible. In the long run, you will produce a consistently flowing and reliable traffic.

4. Have consistency on updating your website.

You must regularly update your website, even one post a week will do. Speaking of traffic generation, consistency is one of the secrets. Visitors are inclined to go back to a website with so much information to get. Doing this will give them the reason not to leave your website. This means, creating new content on regular intervals.

5. Be active and visible on social media sites.

You can create several links back to your websites from social networking sites. The help of social media is a fast way not only for driving traffic but to make leads grow, too. Social media networking sites have lots of community members, most of them are your friends and acquaintances. With that, it is not even difficult to give them a chance to look at your website and endorse it to others.

Today, social media sites are the most active sites everywhere. Get updated with another way of generating traffic through social media sites. Make an account for your service or product and start communicating. Social networking is more of conversation where people discuss almost everything. Search for what your prospects are asking for, and make a post about it.

Considering the above tips for generating traffic is the surest way to boost your success in online business. Start generating your traffic and before you realize it, many visitors have already purchased your product.

Chapter 6:
Factors to Consider When Choosing a Traffic Generation for You

Synopsis

There are a variety of methods to generate traffic to your website these days and it's not hard to become confused and even frustrated when searching for the right one. Although it is not possible to utilize every method there is, but there are some factors you must consider when you are choosing the one that is going to gain you the most recognition.

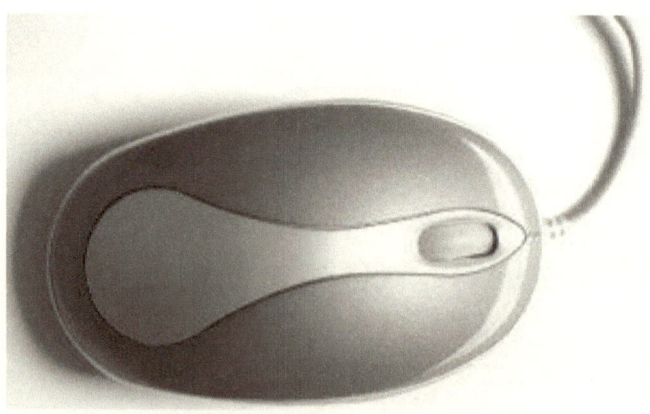

Factors

Who is the Targeted Audience?

Every generation of trafficking will target a specified audience, and they will vary depending on the size and the characteristics. For instance, if you choose to use the more favorable SEO technique, you will be targeting the audience of everybody who utilizes those search engines.

This is a great method for those looking to target a worldwide audience, as everyone uses some kind of search engine when it comes to searching on the web. This is the reason as to why many website owners like the method of SEO, as it targets a very large audience.

How Long Will It Take For the Results to Show?

Depending on what type of method you would like to use, some of them may take a little longer than others for your effort results to actually show.

Take a glance at the article marketing example, this used to be able to produce very immediate results since your articles would land a spot in some of the highest ranking websites almost instantly. Due to recent effects, this method has decreased and it is highly likely that you are going to spend some time waiting for your results to come through.

SEO is one of the methods that requires a lot of time and patience, as it can be very difficult getting a high ranking in the very competitive market. You will have to make sure that your content is perfectly optimized, making sure that all keywords are placed in the right order, and make sure you have plenty of links that point straight to your website, which you will need to keep updated constantly.

One of the newly discovered tactics is called **siphon trafficking**, which is gaining high targeted and quality visitors from authority sites that are found within your target market. Not only are you going to see an immediate boost in your traffic, but you are also going to get some additional benefits from the people who become your visitors. Your links placed on these authority sites to your own can help increase your rankings, while at the same time your small website is gaining tons of recognition thanks to the much larger site.

How Long Will Your Method Serve You?

You need to keep an eye on the efficiency of your trafficking method over a long period of time, this way if you are noticing a decrease in the amount of traffic you have, you can change your method or strategy before your numbers decrease too low.

The main advantage of the siphon trafficking is that your link won't disappear overnight. Those larger websites aren't going to go anywhere meaning you will have a good and stable amount of traffic visiting your site.

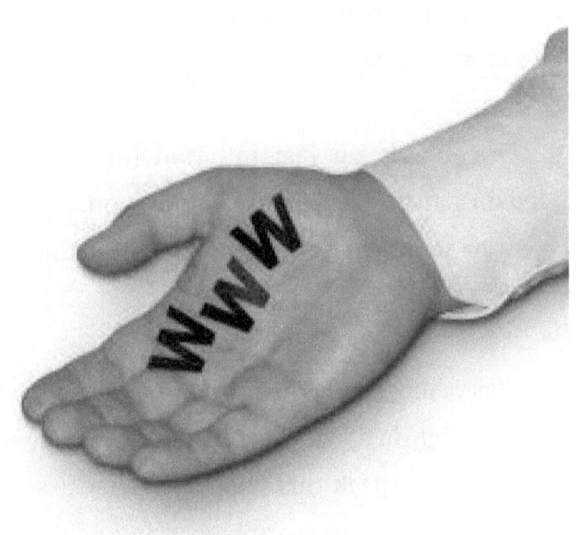

Chapter 7:

Assessment Parameters for a Working Generator

Synopsis

In order to assess our traffic campaign properly certain signals would have to be present to be looked at and analyzed to gauge each campaign's efforts objectively.

Although we can rely on just intuition (as a lot of webmasters), actually looking at the numbers will allow one to see the reality or effectiveness or failures of each component of the traffic generation campaign.

Practically everything can be measured, not all, but a lot. Because we are constantly fighting against the machine which is the search engines so they too speak this language. They assess your rankings based off the same numbers we are analyzing.

Some Metrics of Importance to Look At

Bounce Rates

--Is the ratio or the amount of time a reader spends actually reading the content of your website? The longer the visitor stays, the more the search engines assume you are in possession of quality content. Misleading content results to bad bounce rates of only a few seconds that's tells the spider robots they were misled.

LSI

--Means the thematic or related words and phrases that exist about a certain topic of discussion. If an article is about acai berries but has been misleadingly titled to be about "high definition television" for example, the robots can tell it is not really about televisions but is about the berries because of the words existing within the content.

CTR

--**Click through rates** measure the actual people who visit your site from the number of eyeballs or views from the site. The higher the CTR means the more targeted the quality of traffic is. If the content is about again acai berries and the call to action at the end says "to find out more about high definition television please click here open", they probably do not waste time going there as they are interested in the acai berries. Therefore, lower CTRs and one of the symptoms of poorly targeted traffic.

Page Views

--Measure the raw number of people visiting the website. We cannot determine what their intentions are it's just a raw measurement of visitors. If you want to just get visitors you can create a bunch of traffic generation from many places, from porn to cars whatever it is to jack-up your traffic stats. Some people actually do this when they want to sell their websites to make it appear more attractive for the would-be buyers. There are also bulk traffic sellers on the Internet selling garbage quality traffic for this purpose.

Conversion Rates

--Arguably is the most important metric for a lot of people as this the one that actually pays the bills! Conversion rates can be defined many different ways and it changes directly on whatever CTA (call to action) the website owner wants. If the CTA is to get more email sign-ups then that becomes the conversion. If it is an AdSense site, clicking the ads become the measured conversion to be computed. Same goes for websites trying to sell products so on and so forth.

The Next Step: Using the Information Intelligently

Now knowing just some of the ways to assess traffic and there are plenty more parameters to look at, you can now work on improving on them specifically to get more quantity and quality of the traffic.

If your website gets a lot of page views but fails on the conversion rate and a high bounce rate, then it indicates the traffic is not targeted and work must be done on the websites copy or text.

Chapter 8:

PPC or Content: Which Brings the Most Profit

Synopsis

There are two types of creating traffic for generating income for internet-based businesses – pay per click (PPC) and content. For new businesses and entrepreneurs content would be the hands-down choice for the simple reason that, well, it does not require cash outlay which cannot be said of PPC.

For cash-strapped businesses, any further argument on the matter is moot and academic. However, perhaps it's best to explore the issue more before you make any choices.

Anyway, coming up with a definitive position on which is better for your business does not require rocket science type of knowledge and takes only a few minutes of your time. It simply involves applying a basic formula for calculating return on investment (ROI) which every business does anyway.

How to PPC ROI

To calculate the return in investment (the money you earn from every dollar you invest in your business), you consider four variables: conversion value of each click, the exact number of clicks, and the cost of prompting people to click. The figures you use naturally will be assumptions, but you can make them as realistic as possible by asking people who are employing PPC strategies to produce more business.

The simplest formula for computing ROI is: (sales - cost) / cost) x 100). You must understand that the sales and cost figures are totals for a specific period, say a month.

To illustrate, let's assume the following figures: Per click conversion value – $44, Cost per click - $1, conversion rate – 3%, and 2,000 in a month. The calculation would be like this:

= (((44 x 0.03 x 2000) - (1 x 2000))/ (1 x 2000)) x 100
= (2640 - 2000)/2000 x 100
= 32%

It is a standard belief among financial experts that businesses operating in a 20% or more ROI level are in a pretty good position.

Computing ROI for Content

Computing the ROI for content (blogs, articles, PRs) is more difficult because unlike PPCs which are time-bound, web content is permanent and drives a steady of stream traffic to business websites albeit at a slower rate. However, by considering the differences, it's still easy to come up with an ROI that accurately presents the potential earning capacity of a business relying on organic search to drum up traffic and sales.

Obviously, the conversion rate of content driven program will be a lot lower than the PPC's, so assume a reduced .05% conversion rate, but retain the same $44 conversion value.

You wouldn't be spending for direct ads; your cost will come from researching, writing, posting and promoting your blogs. For every blog, assume you spend four hours. How then do you compute for the cost of each blog? Well, you can probably use the per hour rate you get from your permanent job; let's assume you get $30 per hour. Your cost for each blog will be $120 (4 hours x 30).

Next, we assume the maximum number of page views your blog will get while it's online and since you are probably just an average blogger like most of us, a modest 1,000 for your bog is probably just about right.

Your content ROI is:

Content ROI = (((44 x 0.005 x 1000) - 120) / 120 x 100

= 83%

Which is better?

Just by looking at the ROIs you would instantly conclude that blog or content generated traffic is better. Looking at some other things can help you come to a more a precise conclusion:

1. The blog ROI is lifetime while PPC's ROI covers the period of the campaign.
2. The PPC involved risking $1000 in cash while the blog post did not involve any cost.
3. The PPC ROI did not account for the labor cost of making the ads.

Look at the figures and the considerations, then, decide.

Chapter 9:

The Value of Traffic

Synopsis

The Odd Truth of the Secrets of Traffic Generation on the Web

There might be numerous ways provided for on the web as regards increasing traffic toward your website but none of the ways – save for one or two – can retain that traffic for a long time. This simply means that the methods provided on the internet may only last a month, or if you get lucky, two. For traffic to be generated and to last, the best way possible to do it is to provide content that people want and need.

Countless marketers on the internet fail to see the importance of creating excellent content for their respective websites. They take too much time choosing the best web tools to integrate on their websites instead of taking time to create content that are always searched by online users. With great content, a website will increase its visibility and its reliability that will then directly result to an increase in sales and reputation.

Quality and Value

Ultimately, it does not really matter what topic you have on your website because people are looking for content that can either help them with their current situations or those that could bolster their arsenal of knowledge. Create content that is as flawless as possible and that provides value for your readers to appreciate your work.

Emphasize Solutions and Benefits

Content that solves different, true-to-life problems are hitting the mark on the web because everyone has problems of their own. Now it is your duty to provide proven solutions that can be done by everyone – the rich, the poor, the young and the old.

By this, you can show people that you are not just beating around the bush to generate traffic; you are there to provide answers to questions and solutions to almost all problems.

After you provide proven solutions to particular problems, it would be best o tell your readers why they should try the solution you've shown so that they too may benefit from it.

This is one aspect where most online marketers go wrong because they think that after they have provided the solutions, people will stay and read more about it. That's totally wrong because people or readers for that matter will only stay if you have something more in store for them that is, in one way or the other, useful for them.

Be Real and Show Them the Way

The more you show yourself to your readers, the more they will admire your honesty towards them. It is important for you as the content creator or the website owner, to develop some kind of connection with your readers. This way, you can show them why you are there in the first place – creating content for everyone to read and learn.

After they have an idea of who you really are, you can now start to show them the way to get to the next level of things. To some, this is the hard part of doing things but if you get the vibe of it, you will definitely have a good time whilst providing information for everyone, not to mention generate more traffic to your website.

Wrapping Up
Sample Case Study

In this chapter, everything you have learned so far – and will additionally learn through the case study – will finally be put to the test. Traffic on the basis of SEO alone is like eating the most expensive steak...that got heated in a microwave oven. The quality is still there, but the freshness of its taste, its soul – is gone.

With this case study, you will learn for yourself how to build traffic without just relying on SEO tactics. You'll also be generating traffic simply by building your relationships with other bloggers and marketers in your niche. For this study, commit to perform the following actions for one of your blogs or websites.

Video Responses

You know by now that blog commenting can generate a good amount of traffic. However, aside from posting merely text comments consider responding this time to posts of the top bloggers and marketers in your niches with a *video*. It won't cost you a penny, is easy to do, and is guaranteed to have a huge impact. Bloggers and marketers always appreciate it when other people take the time to go the extra mile for them!

Top (Insert Number Here) Posts

This type of post generates lots of traffic for two reasons.

- Including the word *"Top"* in the title of your post lets readers know that what they're about to read is likely to be essential advice. Words you can use as alternatives include "Best", "Worst", and "Most".

- Having a *number* included in your title is also a good thing because it makes your post quantifiable. People like knowing the *exact* number of ways they can benefit from reading a particular blog post or article. **7** or **10** are always good numbers to have in your title but try not to go below 5 at the very least.

Writing with Personality

Making a connection and building a relationship with other bloggers and marketers do not rely on the content of your posts or comments alone. They must ooze with your great personality as well! With thousands of individuals trying to make it big in niche marketing, cookie-cutter content won't cut it at all.

Contrary to popular opinion, today's most successful bloggers and marketers aren't turned off by peers with strong opinions! Just make sure that you do have a point to make and you're not writing something just to create noise for your site.

Networking

The crème de la crème of the bloggers and marketers in your niche are likely to turn down 99% of the submissions for guest posts in their sites. The best way to catch the attention of a "high roller" is to reverse the process and *make them notice you* instead.

Admittedly, that's easier than done but the sweetest rewards on earth always are. In this case, you just have to be patient and continuously work hard on building relationships with other bloggers and marketers.

Signature Style

Your favorite blogger may be best known for his or her case studies on traffic. Another favorite niche marketer of yours may enjoy massive traffic every time he writes a Top 10 post. It's important that you find your own signature style as this will pave the way to top bloggers knocking on your door and asking for guest posts when – in the real world – it's usually the other way around.

Commit to doing these steps for a specific period of time. See for yourself if the above tips work and if they do, you've got your own case study to explore and share with your readers!

www.ingramcontent.com/pod-product-compliance
Lightning Source LLC
Chambersburg PA
CBHW030537220526
45463CB00007B/2869